Banners
for the
LORD

Written and Illustrated
by Teresa M. Staal-Cowley

WestBow Press books may be ordered through booksellers or by contacting:

WestBow Press
A Division of Thomas Nelson & Zondervan
1663 Liberty Drive
Bloomington, IN 47403
www.westbowpress.com
844-714-3454

ISBN: 979-8-3850-1208-4 (sc)
ISBN: 979-8-3850-1207-7 (e)

Library of Congress Control Number: 2023921358

Print information available on the last page.

WestBow Press rev. date: 11/09/2023

WESTBOW
PRESS®
A DIVISION OF THOMAS NELSON
& ZONDERVAN

Banners for the LORD

1.   May the LORD answer you in the day of trouble!
May the name of the God of Jacob set you securely on high!
2.   May He send you help from the sanctuary and support you from Zion!
3.   May He remember all your meal offerings and find your burnt offering acceptable!

4.   May He grant you your heart's desire and fulfill all your counsel!
5.   We will sing for joy over your victory, and in the name of our God we
will set up our banners. May the LORD fulfill all your petitions.

6.   Now I know that the LORD saves His anointed; He will answer him
from His holy heaven, with the saving strength of His right hand.
7.   Some may boast in chariots, and some in horses; but we
will boast in the name of the LORD, our God.
8.   They have bowed down and fallen, but we have risen and stood upright.
9.   Save, O LORD; May the King answer us in the day we call.

Psalms 20: 1-9, New American Standard Bible,
The Open Bible Edition, Thomas Nelson Publishers.

Art Banners for the LORD

My journey becoming interested in Banners for the LORD began in the year 2000 when I became involved with and soon after as a studio artist with the 101 Artists Colony in Encinitas California. All the artists collaborated and came up with a plan to display 101 Arts Alive Banners that would hang along highway 101 in Encinitas. The finished banners are submitted at the end of the year, unveiled at the beginning of the following year with a ceremony inviting the community to attend and participate. The banners are displayed each year for approximately six months from signposts along highway 101. At the end of the display the banners have been auctioned off, with 50 % going to the artists and the remaining 50 % covering administrative expenses of banners, marketing and renting a cherry picker to hang and take down the banners. Any additional monies are donated to local nonprofit charities. Many tireless, talented artists, and community members, have kept the 101 Artist Colony Arts Alive Banners going.

I created two four feet by eight-foot Arts Alive Banners for the years 2003 and 2004 that were auctioned off. As a Christian artist and calligrapher, I always contemplate and pray about every project I create. It was agreed that the 101 Artist Colony could not support artwork with religious or political content; we had to be nonpartial. However, I always pray for wisdom when I create artwork. December 2004, I moved to Olympia with three of my younger children, my oldest settled in the area shortly after. The father of my children passed away. I remarried in 2008. Professors from The Evergreen State College, adult children and husband encouraged me to create more Arts Alive Banners. I created art banners for the years 2013 and 2020. These art banners were approximately two feet by four feet. For this book I will focus on Banners for the LORD.

California National Day of Prayer Banner May 6, 2004

The San Diego County Chapter of the National Day of Prayer commissioned me to create this Art Banner in 2004 after seeing my Arts Alive Banners I created for the 101 Artists Colony in Encinitas, California. The National Day of Prayer chapter members knew I openly shared my faith as a Christian artist and calligrapher, but that I respected I do not share my faith in the Arts Alive Banners. This was a treasured opportunity as an artist, calligrapher and Christian to create this Art Banner representing the California National Day of Prayer in 2004. The Art Banner was rolled up and unveiled in a ceremony honoring our LORD with Christians in San Diego County and many throughout California. My family and I and many present signed the Art Banner.

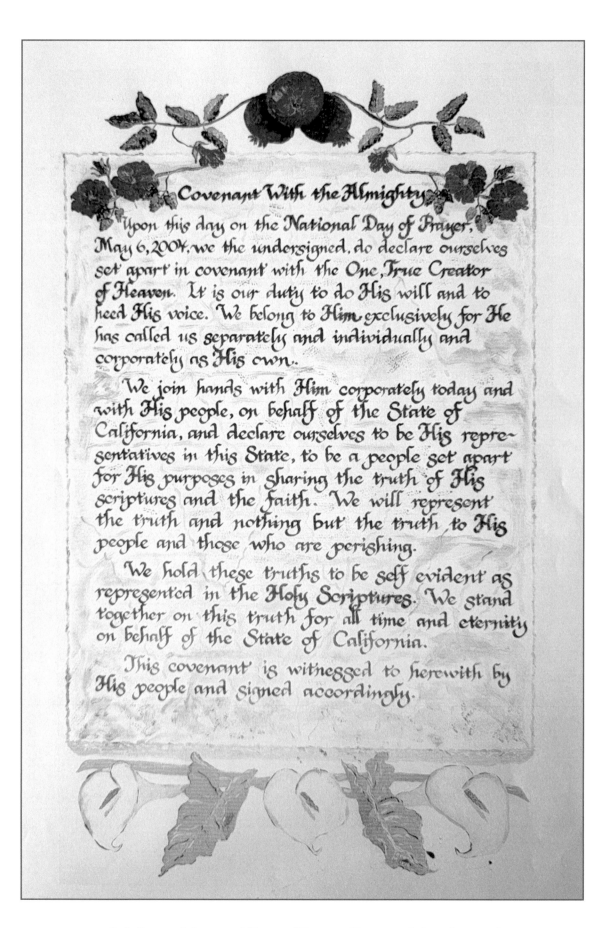

California National Day of Prayer Banner, May 6, 2004

Song of Solomon 2:4

4. "He has brought me to His banquet hall and His banner over me is love." Song of Solomon 2:4, NASB, Hebrew Bible, Old Testament

The inspiration for the Song of Solomon 2:4 Art Banner came because of a dream I had of Jesus telling me specifications of what He wanted me to create. I learned the summer of 2004 to obey when I had a dream of Jesus showing me a raging fire with the words 'Refiners Fire" undulating within. I was encouraged to create for a specific pastor in North San Diego County. I challenged Jesus telling Him I could not create something like that for a pastor who had authority over me. I could not sleep for three nights and felt overwhelmed in what Jesus asked of me. The third sleepless night I created the artwork, framed it, and delivered it to the church office for the pastor, when they opened.

The Song of Solomon 2:4 Art Banner includes images of grapes, figs, pomegranates, pears, almonds, balm of Gilead, olives and branches. The words of the scripture are tossed in the air as a memorial when Jesus came into the Temple and turned over the tables of the money changers.

My youngest child was in middle school at the time when I created the Song of Solomon 2:4 Art Banner. My youngest had twin friends whose parents were Hebrew scholars. The twins were intrigued by the art and told their parents. I was invited to bring the Art Banner to their home and spend Friday night Shabbat with my youngest, the twins and their parents. The Hebrew scholars questioned of how I knew the symbolism and meaning of the scripture, the colors, and images I included. I responded that I did not know, and that Jesus told me to do so in a dream. The Hebrew scholars questioned as to why a Gentile woman would create an Art Banner of this specific type for the Messiah, when they believe the Hebrew Patriarchs will be called to do so when the Messiah comes.

Song of Solomon 2:4, NASB

The Trinity of God, Father, Son, and Holy Spirit

I had a dream with God the Father, Jesus Christ the Son, and Holy Spirit. I perceived God the Father as bright yellow light, Holy Spirit as misty blue atmosphere and Jesus Christ the Son as blood red. Primary colors are yellow, blue, and red much like the Trinity of God are three persons of God in one as the primary colors are individual colors that make up all colors and one in color. God the Father revealed himself as in Genesis 1:1, "In the beginning God created the heavens and the earth." Holy Spirit revealed themself as in Genesis 1:2, "And the earth was a formless and desolate emptiness, and darkness was over the surface of the deep, and the Spirit of God was hovering over the surface of the waters." Jesus Christ revealed Himself as in John 1:1, "In the beginning was the Word, and the Word was with God, and the Word was God." NASB,

Hebrew Bible, Old Testament, New Testament.

Genesis 1:1, NASB

Genesis 1:2, NASB

John 1:1, NASB

For God So Loved The World-West

16. "For God so loved the world, that He gave His only Son, so that everyone who believes in Him will not perish but have eternal life." John 3:16, NASB, New Testament Bible

I created this art banner per the request of a pastor at a church I attended. If you look closely, I painted God's arms and hands with stars as He holds the world in His hands. The plan was originally to paint an art banner of the Western hemisphere. The pastor wanted the first part of the scripture with the words I wrote. After I was finished, I called the pastor to set up a time to show him my finished art. That night I had a dream. In the dream Jesus gave me new ideas to paint another art banner as a companion to the one I finished.

For God So Loved The World-West, John 3:16, NASB

For God So Loved The World-East

16. "For God so loved the world, that He gave His only Son, so that everyone who believes in Him will not perish but have eternal life." John 3:16, NASB, New Testament Bible

The companion art banner Jesus showed me the Eastern Hemisphere and expressed how much He also loved this side of the world too. Jesus reminded me where Paradise once was, where life began in the Garden of Eden, and where the early patriarchs and matriarchs of faith began, where His family lived and where He was born and so much of history immerged. Jesus expressed grief over most of the wars happening in the Eastern hemisphere. The next day I painted this art banner like the first, with the image of God's hands and arms made by the stars holding the world with love and compassion.

For God So Loved The World-East, John 3:16, NASB

I AM the Alpha and the Omega, the First and the Last, the Beginning and the End.

13. "I am the Alpha and the Omega, the first and the last, the beginning and the end."
Revelation 22:13, NASB, New Testament Bible

The Revelation 22;13 Art Banner came as an inspiration when my now husband began hearing about me, we first met in 2006 at an art store. In 2007 he began contacting me taking me out on dates, trying to prove to me that God did not exist and advise me that my life would go better if I stopped being a Christian and stopped creating Christian art. He came from the perspective that he was a nuclear engineer in the Navy, managed nuclear power plants and was a nuclear engineer for the state. The dates over dinner consisted of him talking about spies, Americans committing treason, atoms, neutrons, protons, and electrons, explaining how atomic bombs and nuclear bombs are made, fission and nuclear energy in power plants, writing diagrams on paper napkins and dividing salt and pepper in little piles. He showed me his green antique glass collection that emitted nuclear energy. He shared with me that he did not believe in God and believed in science.

I prayed to God, my LORD for wisdom, for direction, what to say, what not to say, should I stop seeing this man. My LORD gave me the vision portrayed in the Revelation 22:13 Art Banner and said tell him that; "I AM, The Alpha and The Omega, The Beginning and The End, The First and The Last" and I described what Revelation 22:13 looked like. He was shocked, speechless, and responded; "If that is who God is I can believe in Him". He became a Christian and we were married in 2008. In 2010 I created the Art Banner for him as a Christmas gift.

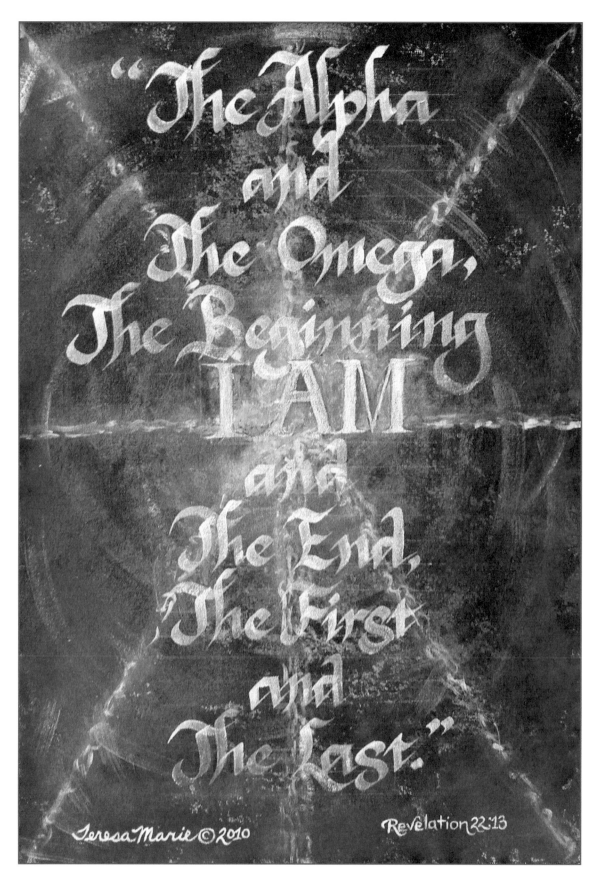

The Alpha and The Omega, The Beginning and The End,
The First and The Last, Revelation 22:13, NASB

I AM the Bread of Life

35. Jesus said to them, "I am the bread of life, the one who comes to Me will not be hungry, and the one who believes in Me will never be thirsty." NASB, New Testament Bible.

I created this art banner as a companion for the art banner "I AM the true Vine". Each of the art banners were created per the request of a pastor at a church I attended that were displayed during the Easter season in the church. I automatically assumed I should paint shafts of wheat. Again, I had a dream that Jesus came to me instructing me to paint seven commonly used grains across the world that are made into bread, one of which is wheat.

I AM the Bread of Life, John 6:35, NASB

I AM the true Vine

1."I am the true vine, and My Father is the vinedresser. 2. Every branch in Me that does not bear fruit, He takes away, and every branch that bears fruit, He prunes it so that it may bear more fruit." NASB, New Testament Bible

The banner "I AM the true Vine" was created as a companion to "I AM the Bread of Life" for an Easter seasonal display in the church I was attending per the request of the pastor. When I originally created the I AM the true Vine banner I painted an arched grapevine with grapes over and around the lettering in a clockwise direction. Afterward while the paint was still wet, I heard Jesus tell me to smear the paint with a wide brush in circular strokes. I gasped, "No Jesus, I worked so hard painting a beautiful grapevine!" His command was too great, and I obeyed. Jesus told me that this is what He is, He is not stationary, He is powerful, He is movement, He is energy, He is God.

I AM the True Vine, John 15:1, NASB

I AM the Way, the Truth, and the Life.

6. Jesus "said to him, "I am the way, and the truth, and the life, no one comes to the Father except through Me." John 14:6, NASB, New Testament Bible

One night while sleeping during the week of an antique show I had a dream of Jesus was holding a plum bob by a string. He told me to create artwork with the image of the plum bob and write in calligraphy His words from John 14:6.

The next morning, I prayed asking Jesus where to find the plum bob, which vendor to approach, where was I to begin and that there were a few hundred vendors. Jesus directed me down one aisle and another until He said to approach the specific vendor. I asked the man If he had a plum bob. He and his wife were a little shocked because she had been asking him to sell his plum bob, but he did not want to. He pulled out a battered cardboard box from below, carefully opened the box and showed me the plum bob. He held the plum bob as carefully as a baby, removing it from the box. He then carefully put the plum bob in the box as if putting a baby back in their crib. The man shared how he used the plum bob in his career as a land surveyor for 35 years. The man was curious about how I would use his plum bob, and did I know what a plum bob was and how it is used. I admitted I did not know. The man explained to me how to use his plum bob. I shared the dream I had that night with Jesus holding his plum bob and told him that I was to create artwork writing Jesus Words.

I created the artwork and displayed it the next year at the same antique show. The man came to our booth looking for me and discovered my artwork. I offered to give him his plum bob back. The man stood in front of my artwork and quietly wept. He said if that is who Jesus is he can believe in Him. He told me to keep the plum bob. He was going back to tell his wife she can stop praying for him to be a Christian. He believed in Jesus now.

I AM the Way, the Truth, and the Life, John 14:6, NASB

Teresa M. Staal-Cowley

Printed in the United States
by Baker & Taylor Publisher Services